YOU'RE GROUNDED

An Anti-Self-Help
Book to Calm You
the F*ck Down

SWAN HUNTLEY

A TarcherPerigee Book

I would like to dedicate this book to the parts of you that want to be still.

tarcherperigee

an imprint of Penguin Random House LLC
penguinrandomhouse.com

TarcherPerigee with tp colophon is a registered trademark of Penguin Random House LLC

Most TarcherPerigee books are available at special quantity discounts for bulk purchase for sales promotions, premiums, fund-raising, and educational needs. Special books or book excerpts also can be created to fit specific needs. For details, write: SpecialMarkets@penguinrandomhouse.com.

Library of Congress Cataloging-in-Publication Data
Names: Huntley, Swan, author.
Title: You're grounded: an anti-self-help book to calm you the f*ck down / Swan Huntley.
Description: New York: TarcherPerigee, Penguin Random House LLC, 2024.
Identifiers: LCCN 2023044376 | ISBN 9780593715215 (trade paperback)
Subjects: LCSH: Self-realization. | Mind and body.
Classification: LCC BF637.S4 H867 2024 | DDC 158.1—dc23/eng/20240130
LC record available at https://lccn.loc.gov/2023044376
p.   cm.

Printed in the United States of America
1st Printing

Hello.

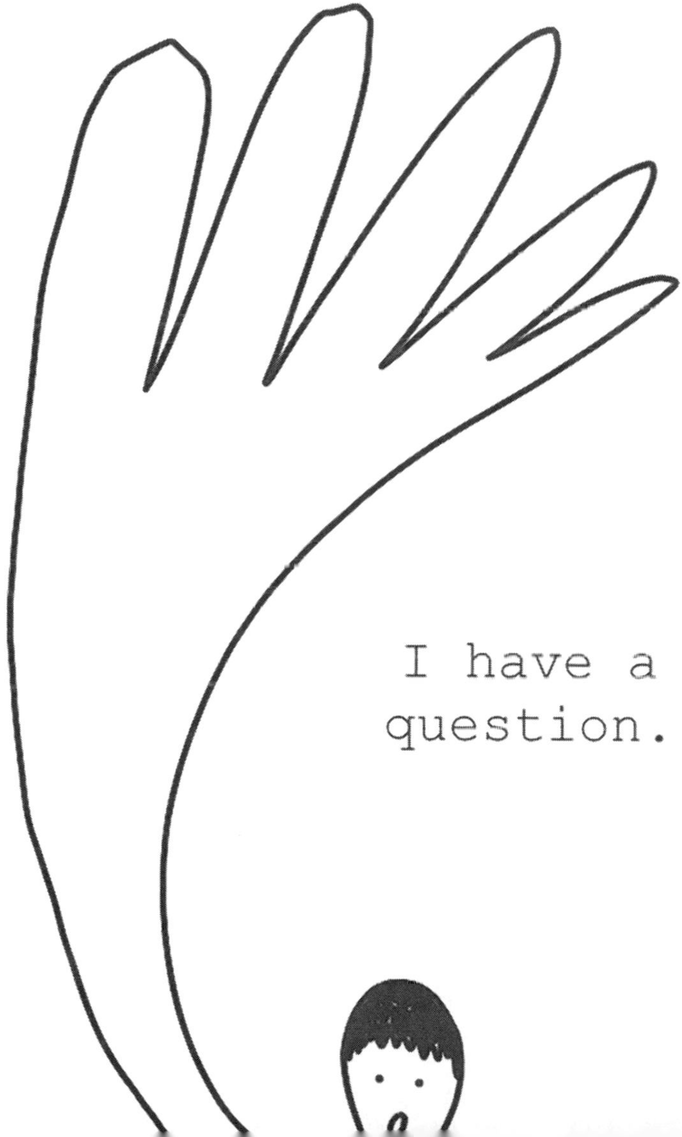

I have a question.

Where are you right now?

Are you here?

Or are you sort of somewhere else?

Please look
at the
ground.

Look closer.

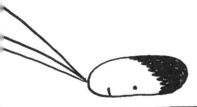

Soon your head will
start floating away.

When that happens,
please return your
gaze to the ground.

And
notice
all the
parts
of your
body
that are
touching
the
ground.

And inhale.

As you
exhale,
imagine
those
parts
sinking
deeper
into
the
ground

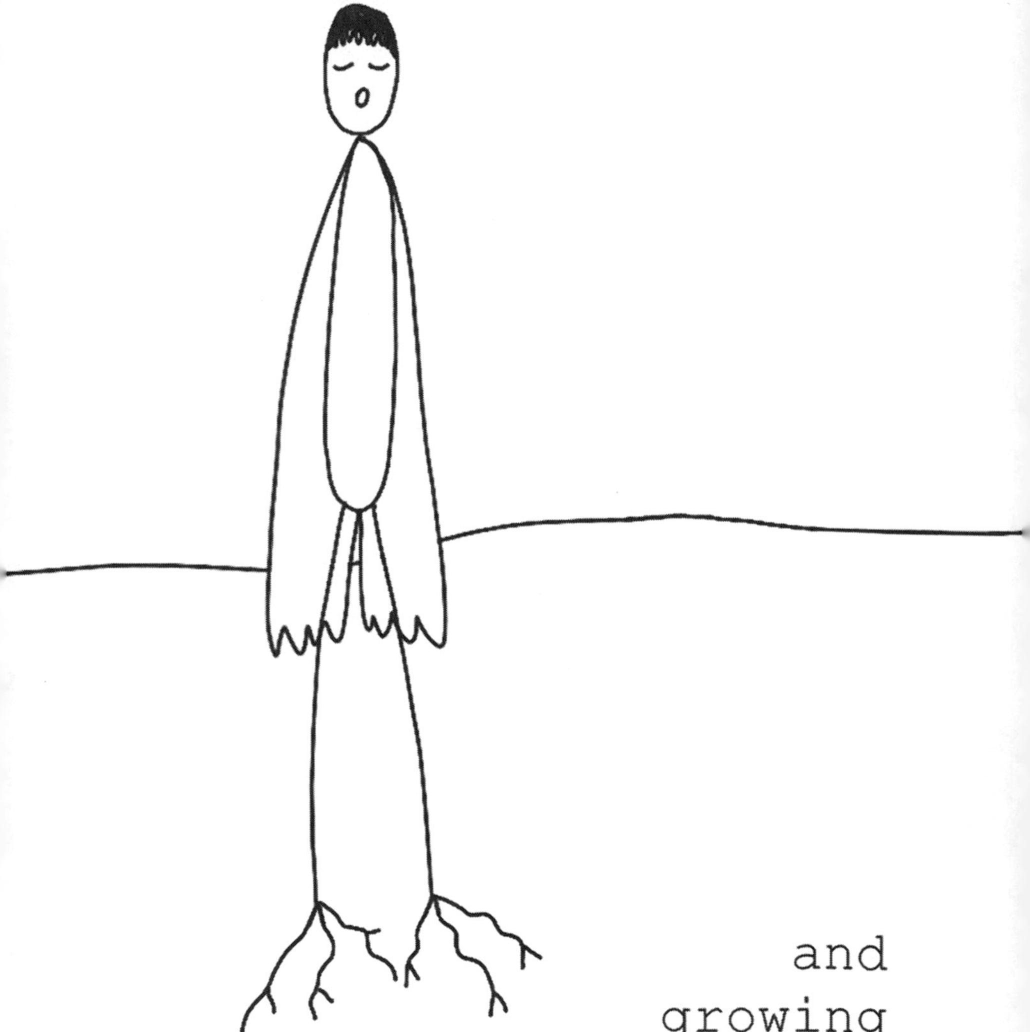

and
growing
roots

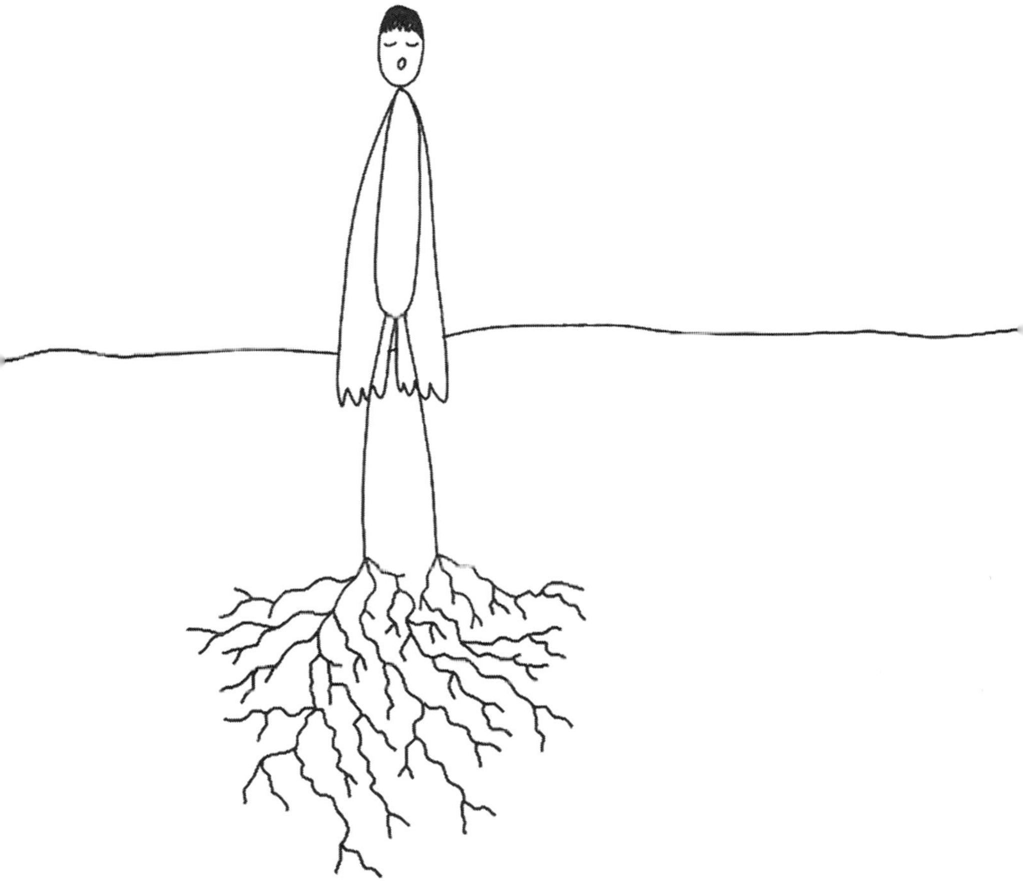

and
spreading

and
wrapping
their root-
fingers
around the
soil

and say to yourself:

This is where I am.

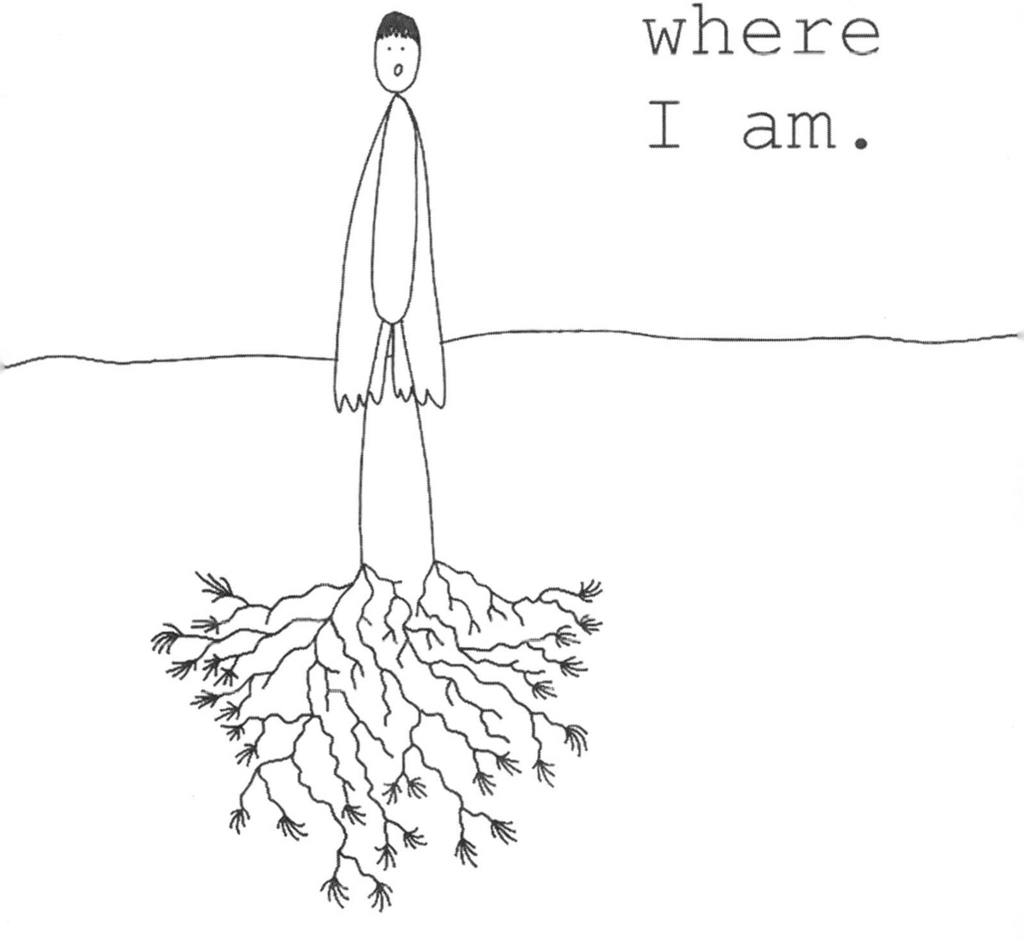

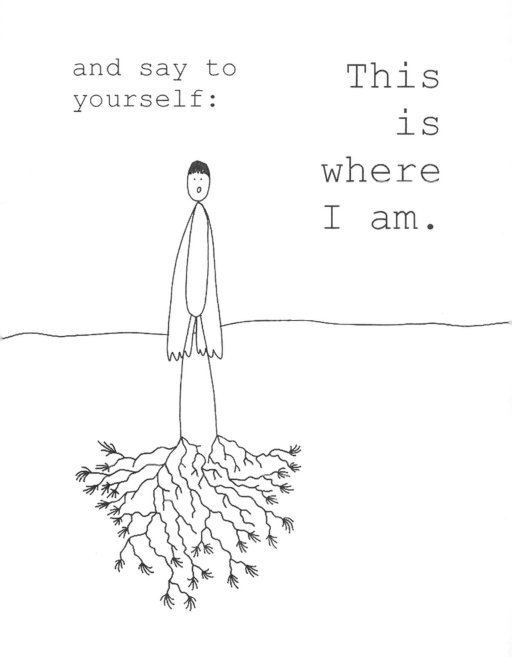

Since most of life is,
on its surface,
mundane, noticing
where you are might
not seem very exciting
at first.

That's normal.

As a species, we seem to believe that unless we're riding a roller coaster or making out with someone on a beach or doing something else that would happen in a toothpaste commercial, then life is lackluster.

I'm now going to solve
all your problems in
one statement:

If you are paying
attention to the
details, then nothing
will ever be
lackluster again.

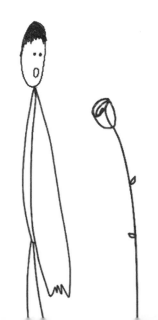

A scenario:

You're staring at a tree.

You've seen so many trees by this point in your life that your reaction to this tree is basically nonexistent.

Actually,
you're
not even
looking
at the
tree.

You're
looking
at your
phone.

Then a blast of
sunlight hits the
leaves for just a
flash and you think:

Oh, that was
kind of
beautiful.

In the seconds after
that, the light
changes again, and
then again, and again.

Every second, until
the end of time, the
light changes.

Here's what I'm trying
to tell you:

This moment will never
happen again.*

*Which is why I don't understand the term
"fleeting moment." Aren't they all fleeting?

A DISCLAIMER BEFORE WE CONTINUE

I'm going to ask you to do a bunch of things in this book that might make you question my authority. I can see you reading a prompt and muttering, "Who is this Susan* chick anyway?"

*Or Sean, which is what the principal called me at my 5th grade graduation ceremony. He said, "Sean Huntley," and my friend said, "I think that's you."

A PROMISE BEFORE WE CONTINUE

If you do what I say,
you will receive a
gift* at the end.

*Let's call it your graduation present.

Did you get all that?

Cool. Moving on.

Have you ever noticed
how many sayings we've
invented about what's
"in the details"?

God is in the details.

The devil's in the
details.

Success is in the
details.

Here's what I think is
in the details:

Beauty.

If you can look beyond
the mundane surface of
things and see beauty,
well, I think that's
what it means to be
fully alive.

Right now I'm sitting at a wooden table in California. In front of me I see two notebooks, a pair of tortoiseshell reading glasses, and an old-school, battery-operated timer. The air feels chilly even though the heat is on. It's quiet, quiet, quiet, and then a car swooshes by. My neck hurts. The air smells like clean laundry. The light is hollow but friendly.

Where are you right now?

Please write about it below.

Please draw a tree and stare
at it for 10 seconds.

If you actually did that, I'm glad.

If you thought, "I am smarter than this prompt," and skipped it, then please return to the previous page and write:

I am smarter than this prompt, but I'm going to suspend my judgment and do it anyway.

Then suspend your judgment and do it anyway.

ANOTHER DISCLAIMER
BEFORE WE CONTINUE

In order to be
present, you have to
want to be present.

I know that sounds
obvious, but I find
that the more
complicated we make
things, the further we
get from the truth.

I have this theory
that a lot of us want
to be present because
we've heard that's
what we should want,
but we haven't really
thought about it
beyond that.

Why do you care about being
present?

What percentage of the time are you present?

What percentage of the time do you think you should be present?

What percentage of the time do you think you will be present after reading this book?

When I leave the
present moment, there
are two places I go...

1. THE PAST

sea of regret

I shouldn't have
complimented that
fugly dress.

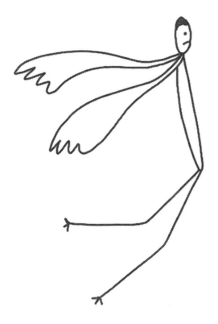

Go to sleep.
It's 2 AM.

2A. THE FUTURE (FANTASY)

Everybody*
loves me.

**

*Specifically older women who remind me of my mother.

**My fantasies about the future are loudest when I'm jogging, because that's when I feel most like the star of a toothpaste commercial.

2B. THE FUTURE (FEAR)

It's 2 AM again and
I'm here to remind
you that you're about
to lose everything
you have and not get
anything you want.

Of course, we all take trips to the past and the future every day.

We have memories.

Ha ha ha, remember
when I complimented
that fugly dress?

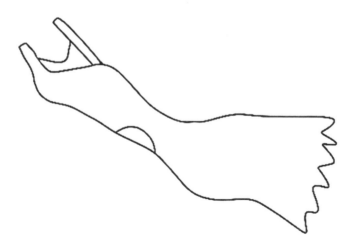

We set goals.

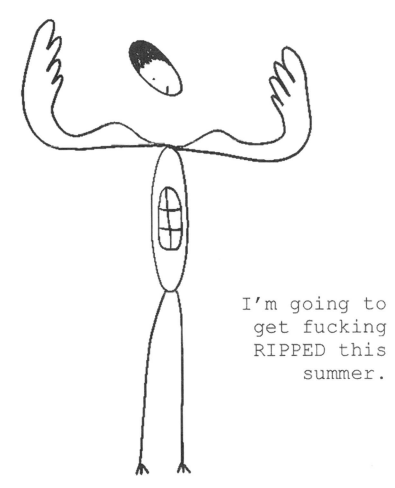

I'm going to get fucking RIPPED this summer.

And this is wonderful
as long as:

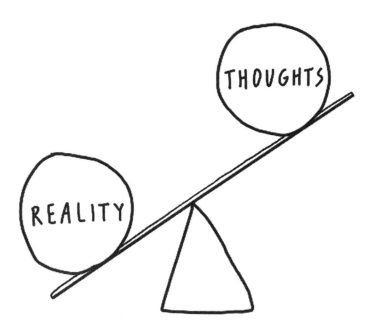

When anything becomes
more real than
reality, then you have
lost the plot.

You have also lost
your body.

Sometimes I think we
live in a world of
floating heads

and forgotten bodies.

The last time you got stuck
in the past, what were you
thinking about?

The last time you got stuck in
the future, what were you
thinking about?

Okay cool, so now
take all the
fantasies, fears, and
regrets you just wrote
about and put them in
this box.

Thoughts that
are trying to
eat me alive

Did that bum you out?

If so, put your hand
over your heart and
say to yourself:

Hi.

And now please draw another
tree and stare at it for 30
seconds.

Once upon a time, at a
restaurant in a cold
city, I looked out the
window and thought:

If I go outside and
smoke a cigarette,
then I will be more
comfortable than I am
now.

Five minutes later,
there I was speed-
smoking in the frigid
night, thinking:

If I go back inside,
then I will be more
comfortable than I am
now.

I had ditched my dinner companion (who resembled a goose) to go on this little merry-go-round, and when I got back to the table, I made a confession:

In every moment, I'm thinking about how I can be comfortable in a future moment.

This was circa 2006 when I had long hair.

Here's what I wanted
my dinner companion to
say:

Me too.

Here's what she said:

I don't
think
that's
good.

After I swallowed the "Holy shit, are we not all having the same experience of being alive?" lump in my throat, I said:

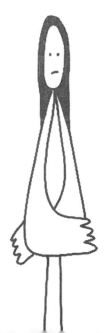

But the problem is that whenever I get to the more comfortable place, it's never as comfortable as I wanted it to be.

The other
problem is that
escaping the
present moment
takes me
further away
from true
comfort.

Here's what I do a
lot:

I build an
oasis in my
mind.

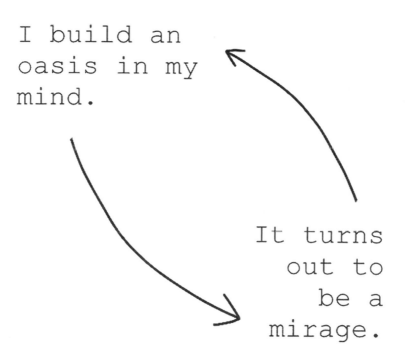

It turns
out to
be a
mirage.

This means that I am
endlessly crawling
through the desert of
my life, refusing to
believe that this is
it.

Do you know what I'm
going to say next?

This
is
it.

Below, please draw another tree and next to it write, "I surrender." Then stare at it for 45 seconds.

Every time you see a
tree after this, I
want you to think
about how big nature
is and how small you
are, and then I want
you to mumble to
yourself, "I
surrender."

I think we could say
that the opposite of
surrender is
attachment so...

POP QUIZ

This is your hand. Is
it reaching for
something or letting
something go?

Isn't it funny how
those two actions look
the same physically?

I think it's
hilarious.

Please tell me about a moment
in your life when you were
incredibly present. Write
down everything you remember.

Now please describe a moment
in which you wish you'd been
more present—without being a
dick to yourself about it.

Please inhale like you mean it.

On the exhale, let out a Brian.

Okay, I meant to write "groan," but I'm feeling like going with the flow so I'm leaving "Brian."

Your Brian might sound like this:

UGGGHH!

Cool. So doing that
stimulates your vagus
nerve, which you can
think of as the
vibrational string
that attaches your
head to your body.

Brian?

When you
exhale with
sound, you
are returned
to yourself.

Are you noticing a
theme here?

The answer, when you
drift out of the
present moment, is not
intellectual.

It's physical.

Maybe we could even
say it's
gravitational.

It's to remember that
you have a body

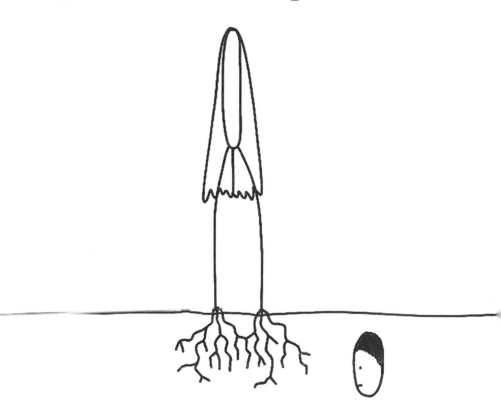

and that your body
belongs to the earth.

Theoretically, life is
simple.

You're just a mammal
who happens to be

breathing
breathing
breathing

and still breathing.

But life is not simple
because you keep
filling the box

Thoughts
that are
trying to
eat me
alive

with complicated
problems that aren't
actually complicated
and might not even be
problems.

Here's the point I'm
trying to make, Brian:

It makes total sense
that we want to
escape.

Once in a while, I
walk from East LA to
the beach (it's far),
and every time, I
think:

Am I literally
trying to walk
away from myself
right now?

Some observations that occur to me on long walks:

My enemy seems to be stillness.

My ongoing suspicion seems to be that something is missing.

My default belief seems to be that I should exist, but not fully.

And meanwhile, the modern world is constantly presenting me with things I think I need in order to feel better.

Here are 10 of my faves:

1. COFFEE

I would sleep through
my life without you.

2. SHOPPING

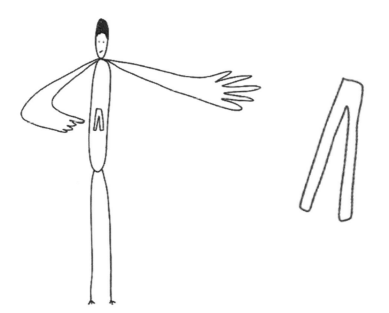

The perfect pair of
white jeans will fill
the hole in my soul.

3. WORK

If I don't
succeed, I'll
die penniless
and alone under
a bridge.

4. WORKING OUT

The real
reason I'm
getting
RIPPED this
summer is so
that people
will be like,
"Wow, you're
definitely
worth my
time."

These next three
favorite escapes are
in the cemetery
because I abused them
so profoundly that I
had to kill them off.

5. SUGAR

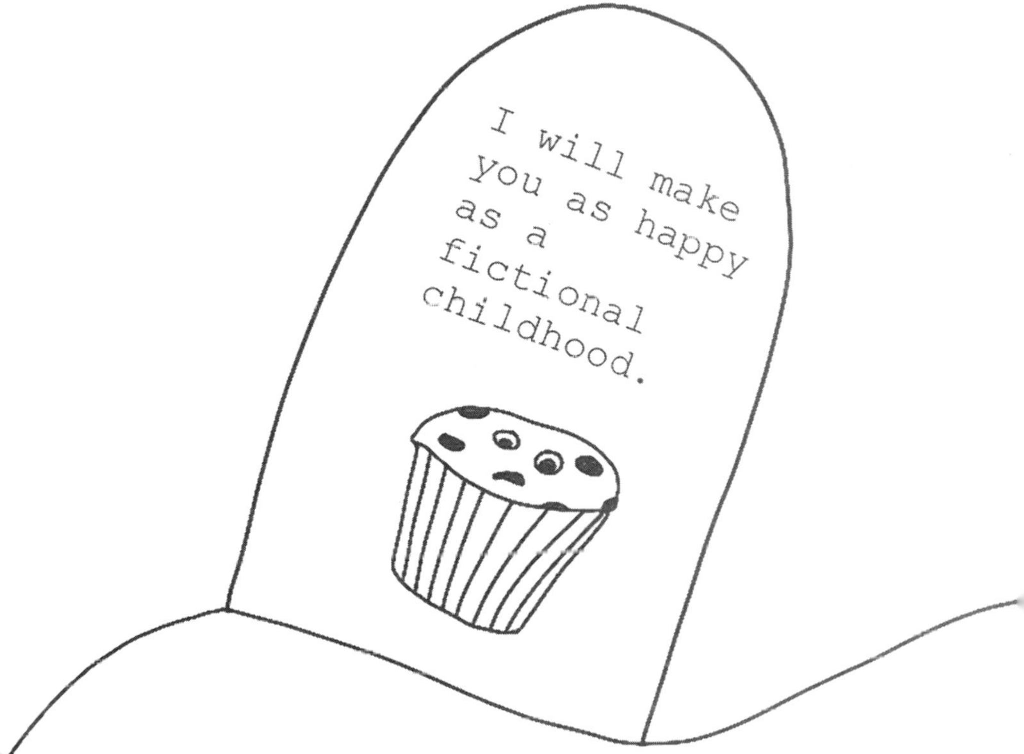
I will make you as happy as a fictional childhood.

6. SMOKING + VAPING

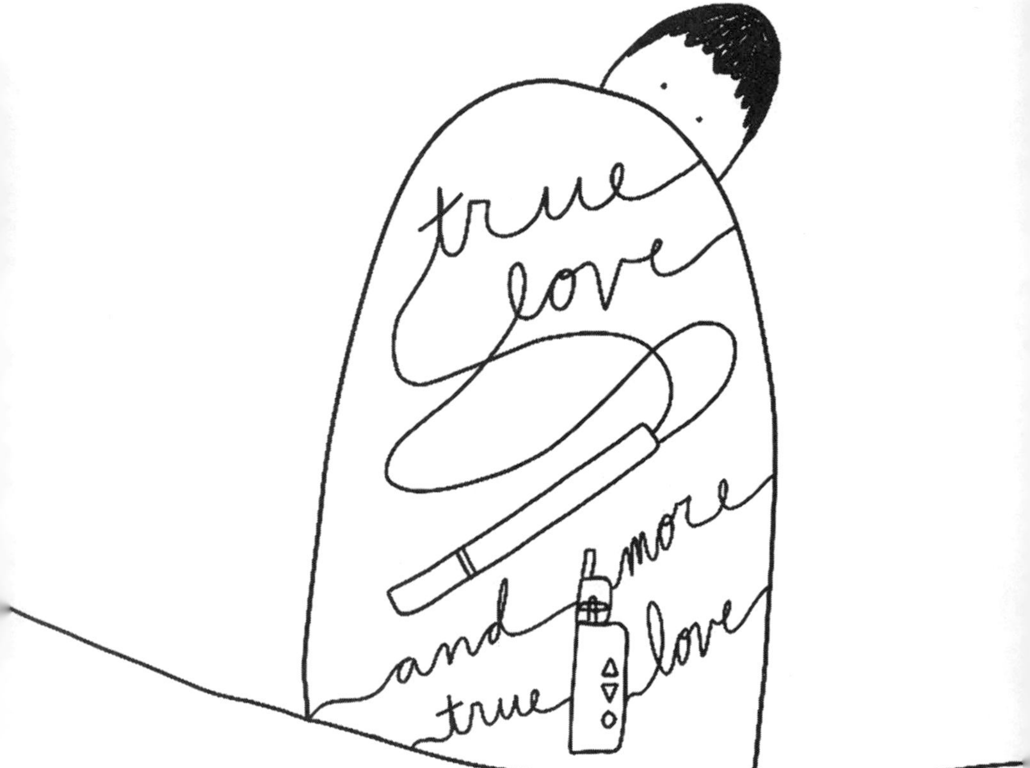
true love
and more true love

7. DRINKING + DRUGS

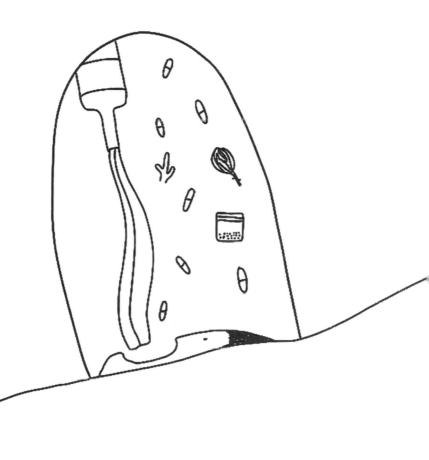

Before we move on, I'm
wondering: What do you reach
for when you want to feel
better?

How does it make you feel to be talking about this?

Please draw another tree and
stare at it for 1 minute.

Let's break down in
more detail the last 3
things my inner
emptiness yearns for.

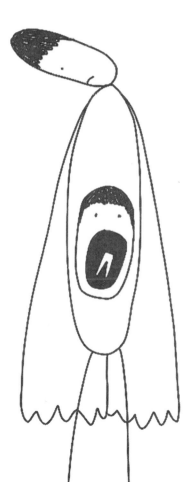

8. THE LOVE OF EVERY SINGLE PERSON ON EARTH

I want acquaintances to give me trophies for existing, I want strangers to check me out on the street, I want all people to love me.

Yes, this includes the people who I don't even like.

You might be thinking
that the desire to be
loved by all is
nonsensical and
unrealistic.

I'm thinking that too.

And yet, I keep
handing people my
heart and saying:

I expect everything
from you.

Who in your life do you hope
will change soon? If they do
change, how will you feel? If
they don't change, how will
you feel?

Please imagine the
person you want to
change. Shrink them
down to the size of a
match. Place them
gently but firmly on a
pretty silver platter.

Now watch as brilliant
gold smoke encircles
this person and
carries them up to the
sun.

Do you feel better?

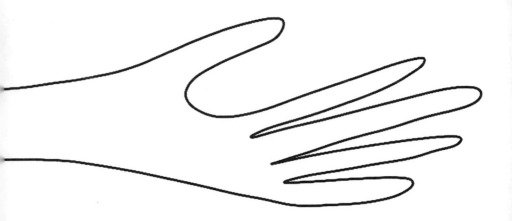

I hope so, because
whomever you let go
of is free now, and
you're free too.

Forging ahead to the
next offender on this
playlist of my
favorite escapes...

9. THE PHONE

POP QUIZ

When was the last time
you went to the
bathroom without your
phone?

Recently, I clicked on an Instagram video of a baby with crazy-wide eyes.

Like, according to this baby's eyes, the world is about to end.

I thought it was so
funny that I clicked
on another baby video,
and then another and
another, and do you
want to know how much
time I spent doing
this?

Literally 2 hours.

The next day, while I was living my real life, I was thinking about my baby friends on Instagram. And I was talking about them too.

So many babies out there are eating cake like drunk people.

But my real life friends didn't care about my baby friends. When I sent them the videos, almost no one responded.

The following night, I
told myself I would
read a book, but then
I spent hours with the
babies again.

I woke up feeling
hungover.

You know how Angelina Jolie has that tattoo in Latin that translates to:

WHAT
NOURISHES
ME
DESTROYS
ME

This was like that. At first the babies brought me joy, but then they stole my peace.

When does your phone stop
bringing you joy? What do you
do when that happens?

Here's what I have
come to understand
about my phone:

It is as
powerful as
a tornado.

And I am as powerful
as one of Angelina
Jolie's eyelashes.

Sometimes, the only way to win is to remove myself from the battle.

What this actually means:

I delete Instagram at least once a day.

And when I really need to concentrate...

I TURN OFF THE PHONE.

You know what happens
shortly thereafter?

I touch the screen and
nothing happens.

And then I remember
that oh yeah, my best
friend / lover / god
The Phone is taking a
nap.

Please turn off your
phone.

You didn't do it, did
you?

Let's try this again.

For just 5 minutes of
your life, please turn
off your phone.

Do you feel how
powerful you are now?

You are the tornado
and your phone is one
of Angelina Jolie's
eyelashes.

Draw another tree. Stare at it
for the remaining few minutes
that your phone is off.

Were you thinking
about The Phone that
whole time?

I know. The separation
is hard.

You can wake her back
up now.

Okay, drumroll please,
because we've arrived
at my final favorite
escape from the
present moment...

10. SELF-IMPROVEMENT

One of my hobbies is to avoid
myself by making lists of ways
in which I plan to improve in
the future.

Sometimes I use planning to improve as a placeholder for actual improvement.

This is because:

(a) honestly shifting a pattern is really, really hard, and

(b) I need something negative to talk about at cocktail parties.

Imagine you're at a
beautiful vista.

You say to your
friend:

                                    Wow.

Your friend says back:

Yeah.

Now imagine an asshole
named Brian broke your
friend's heart.

          I always hated Brian.

Why didn't you tell me?

Let's throw eggs at his house.

I think that's a crime.

          What's the punishment?

Probably a fine.

          Perfect.

When something bad is
happening, the convo
is meaty, because you
have a problem to fix.

I think some people
spend their entire
lives fixing things
that might not even be
wrong just to avoid
the unexciting "wow" /
"yeah" dialogue at the
beautiful vista.

I used to know a self-help fanatic whose life never got better. She liked to read inspirational books and go to personal development conferences and of course she was in therapy. The more time she spent looking for problems, the more problems she found.

I think what kept her going were the epiphanies.

Every time she had one, she seemed like she was on drugs.

Aha!

Let me show you the
value of an epiphany:

 TINY SPECK WORTH
ALMOST NOTHING

Now let me show you
the value of shifting
a pattern:

HUGE, RARE BLOB

The real bummer about my self-help fanatic friend was not that she subsisted on epiphany-crumbs and never really changed.

The real bummer was that she spent all this time gaining wisdom, and then she turned the wisdom into a knife and stabbed herself with it.

REVEAL:

I am the self-help
fanatic friend.

My mask
and wig

And this is my spin cycle:

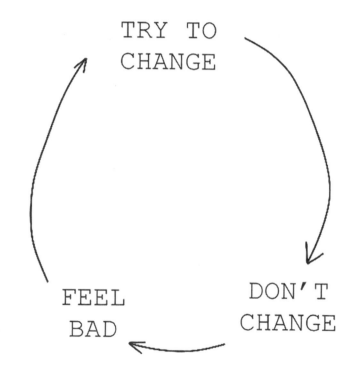

TRY TO CHANGE

DON'T CHANGE

FEEL BAD

Feeling bad might
sound bad at first,
but actually it feels
good, because...

feeling bad is another
escape.

How much time do you spend
thinking about how you want to
change?

How much time do you think you
should spend thinking about
how you want to change?

How much do you expect to evolve in your lifetime? Do you think you will die as a very different person from who you are now?

What patterns have you
honestly shifted so far?

Let's pause and ask a basic
question.

How are you feeling right now?

My guess is that 50%
of you answered, "I'm
tired," and the other
50% of you answered,
"I'm fine...just
tired."

I have this theory
that a lot of us are
drowsy, because we are
sleep-living.

We take the same roads
to the same places, we
eat the same foods, we
stare at clouds out
the same windows.

The repetition alone isn't the problem, for two reasons, which I will express as equations:

1. Routine = structure
2. Structure = good

The problem is that we stop noticing how the roads curve and how the foods taste and how the sky is never the same.

What parts of your life are
you rolling through on
autopilot?

Here's a simple trick,
which I find weirdly
hard to accomplish:

Tweak a routine.

If you eat a vegan
hummus sandwich every
day for lunch, try
adding a few cucumber
slices to it tomorrow.

!!!

Or, if you're writing
a book in which you
mention food, suddenly
decide to make it all
vegan so you can push
the agenda of, you
know, THE ANIMALS.

!!!

I have another basic question.

Why do you think it's so hard
to sit still?

Here's my answer:

Fear of death.

When we are still and
quiet and there's
nothing to listen to
but the sound of our
own breath, we are
reminded that we are
just mammals* who
happen to be alive
right now.

*You might be asking, "What kind of mammals
are these?" And I might be saying, "Any kind
you want, baby."

Right next to "I am
alive" is always her
ruthless twin sister,
"I am going to die."

Death is the ultimate reality.

If your reaction to that is to eat a plate of brownies or read a book about how to be more productive or go on an elaborate quest to find the perfect pair of white jeans...

I understand.

POP QUIZ

Do you meditate?

ANSWER

Yes, all the time you spent staring at trees in this book was you meditating.

I've noticed that when
the word "meditation"
comes up, a lot of
people sprint out of
the room, which is why
I decided to not be
totally honest with
you about what we were
doing.

Do you remember how in the beginning of this book, I mentioned an old-school, battery-operated timer?

I use that to time my meditations. If I use my phone, I look at Instagram just before I start and then I end up meditating about babies.

What's your meditation routine?

If you don't have one, please lie to me.

Cool, so whatever you wrote?

Start doing that tomorrow.

I just realized that
it's going to be hard
to sit quietly if you
feel like you're at
war with yourself.

I guess the answer to
that is love.

If loving yourself
seems out of reach
right now, then please
imagine me, a stranger
in California named
Susan, loving you.

Let's pause and send some love to all the other people who bought this book.

You just received so
much love.

Did you feel it?

POP QUIZ

Who would you be if
you believed the world
was full of beauty?

Are you thinking about
the beautiful things
around you now?

Or are you thinking,
"Where is the gift
Susan promised me?"

Now listen, your first
reaction to this gift
might be, "WHAT?!?"

After you think about
it for a beat, though,
you're going to see
that it's perfect.

My gift to you is this moment.

Here you are, right
now, just breathing.

There's nowhere better
you could possibly be.

Welcome home.

As an homage to the circle, aka the shape of life, let's end this book where we began.

Soon your head will
start floating away.

When that happens,
please return your
gaze to the ground.

And
notice
all the
parts
of your
body
that are
touching
the
ground.

And inhale.

As you
exhale,
imagine
those
parts
sinking
deeper
into
the
ground

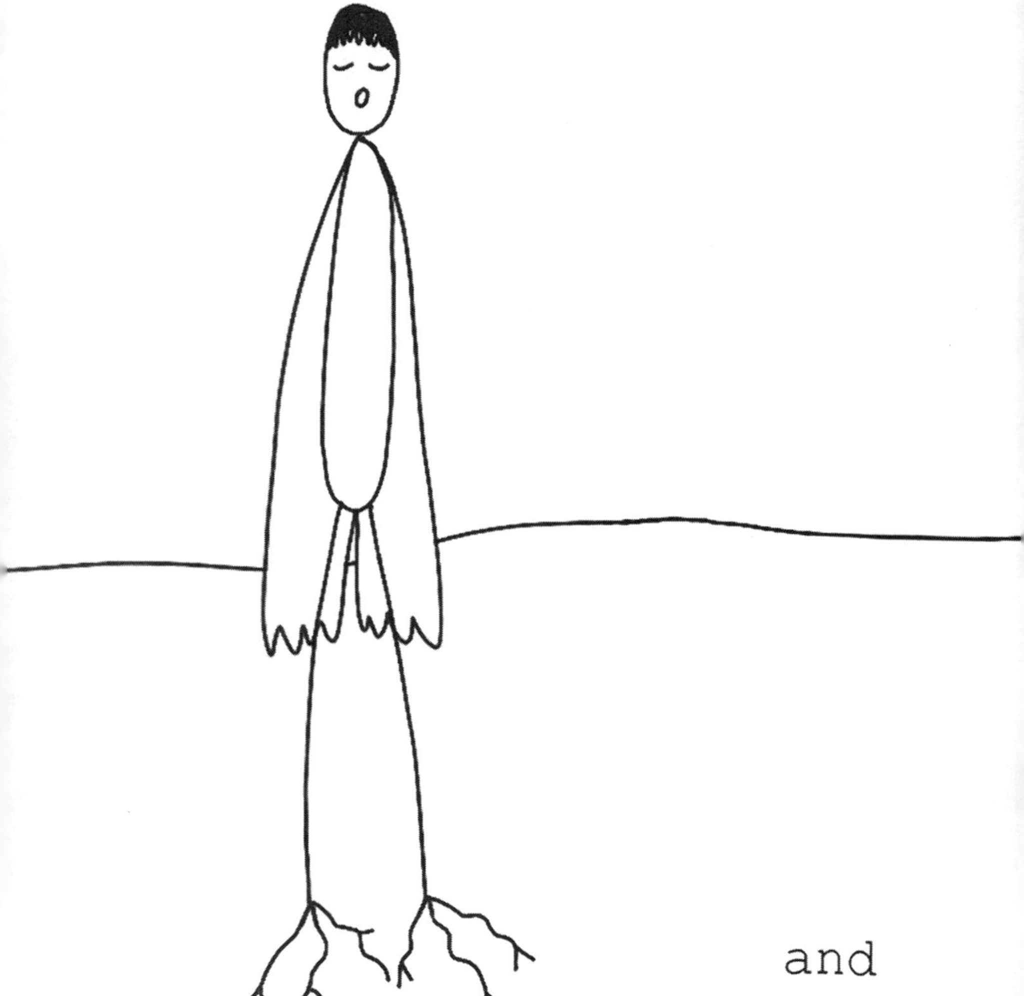

and
growing
roots

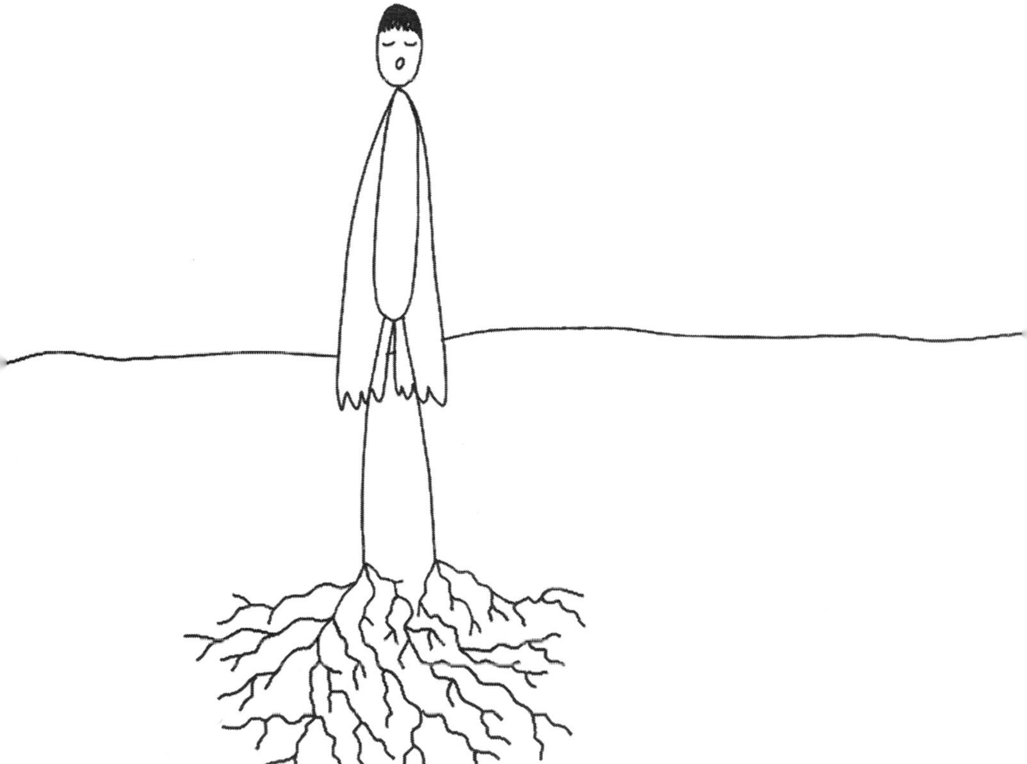

and
spreading

and
wrapping
their root-
fingers
around the
soil

and say to yourself:

This is where I am.

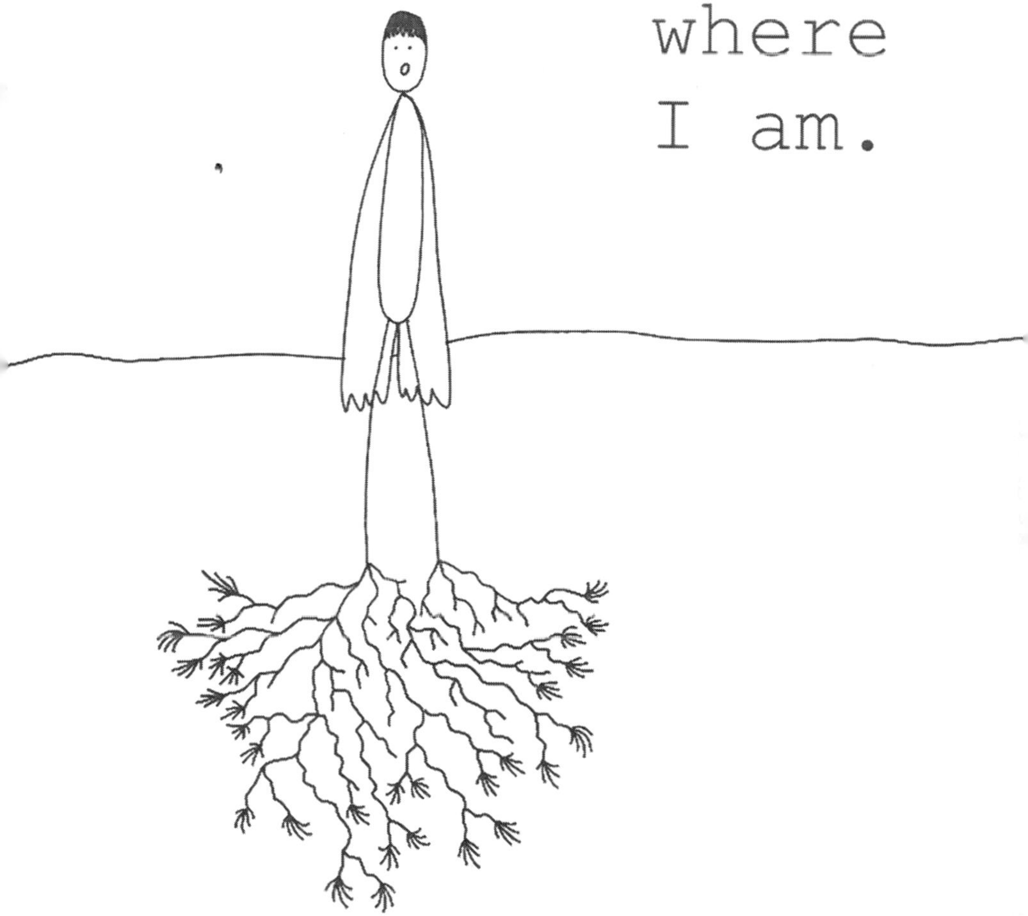

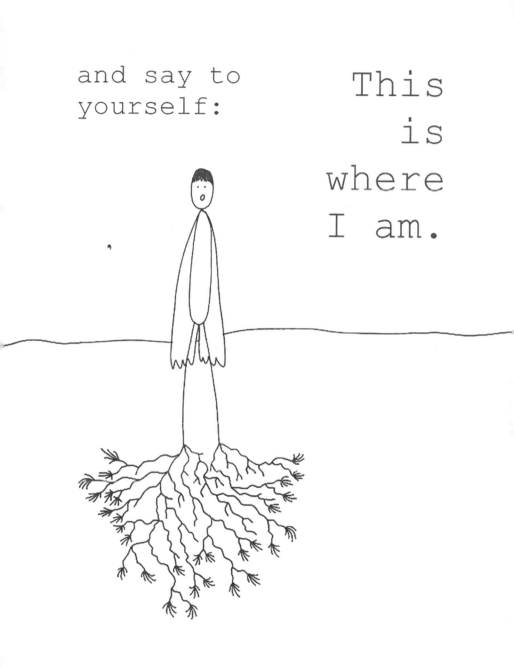

POP QUIZ

What do you belong to?

ANSWER

The earth.

When you forget that
again, go outside, look
at a tree, and surrender.

Thank you to Nora,
Lauren, Fletcher,
Sara, and Rhodes.